Sooner or Later

Sooner or Later

Poems by

Jane Blanchard

Cover design by Shay Culligan
Cover art by Alice Bailly, *Tea Time,* 1920

ISBN: 978-1-63980-133-6

Kelsay Books
502 South 1040 East, A-119
American Fork, Utah 84003
Kelsaybooks.com

To Jimmy

Acknowledgments

Poems in this collection have first been published as follows:

Academic Questions: "Rembrandt"
Algebra of Owls: "Rate"
Anglican Theological Review: "Meeting at the Sewanee Inn"
Artemis: "Annulment"
The Asses of Parnassus: "Accommodation" – "At the Cincinnati Zoo" – "The Brouhaha Re: Panama" – "Detritus" – "A Question of Critique" – "Rhyme after Rime" – "RIP, Antonin Scalia"
Better Than Starbucks: "Admonition"
Blue Unicorn: "Voice Mail"
The Dark Horse: "Nest"
The Dead Mule School of Southern Literature: "Contra Naturam" – "Cut" – "dos-à-dos"
First Things: "All We Like Sheep"
The French Literary Review: "Weavings"
The Kerf: "Faith"
Light: "Mama Drama" – "Railings" – "Strategy"
Lighten Up Online: "Another Spring" – "From the Palace" – "In Toto" – "Just Saying" – "Poetess"
The Listening Eye: "Papier-Mâché"
Mezzo Cammin: "Relic" – "Storage"
Orbis: "Cotillion" – "Living Will"
The Penwood Review: "At Church on Christmas Day" – "By and By"
The Perch: "Ordeal"
The Poetry Porch: The Sonnet Scroll: "Belatedly, a Sonnet"
Poetry Salzburg Review: "Au Naturel"
Quatrain.Fish: "Post-Op"
Reflections: Seasons: "Jive Dive"
River Poets Journal: "Old New World"
The Road Not Taken: "Abode"
The Rotary Dial: "Ipso Facto" – "Testament"

The Seventh Quarry: "Knowledge" – "Quid Pro Quo"
Ship of Fools: "Hiatus"
Shout Them from the Mountain Tops II: "Memoir"
SLANT: "Foregone"
Smoky Blue Literary and Arts Magazine: "Woman of Uncertain Age"
Snakeskin: "André Bénard" – "Artificial Intelligence" – "Comparison" – "Faute de Mieux"
The Tau: "Chanel" – "Ossuary"
Third Wednesday: "Otology" – "Willy-Nilly"
TRINACRIA: "Historicism" – "Pathos"
Vita Brevis: "Natural Disaster"
Website of the Society of Classical Poets: "*Britannia*" – "Dear George," – "Drill" – "Hegemony"
WestWard Quarterly: "Out of the Bag"
You Are Here: "Manifesto"

Poems in this collection have been republished as follows:

Extreme Formal Poems: "Otology"
Families and Other Fiascoes: "Strategy"
Flip Sides: "Belatedly, a Sonnet" – "Ipso Facto"
The French Literary Review: "André Bénard"
The Rotary Dial: "Ipso Facto"
The Shepherd's Voice: "All We Like Sheep" – "At Church on Christmas Day"

"Forthwith" was set to music by James Nord and first sung during the Festival of Nine Lessons and Carols at the Church of the Good Shepherd in Augusta, Georgia, on December 11, 2016.

Contents

"Remember not the former things,
nor consider the things of old."

Isaiah 43:18

Poetess

The Muse has come to visit me,
So I must entertain—
If she should be dissatisfied,
I shall write verse in vain.

Some English tea and ginger cake
Might suit her taste just fine—
Perhaps she will not notice that
The silver needs a shine.

Relic

The antique cup had shattered when it fell.
With pieces found and glued together, it
Appeared almost unbroken. Rather well
It sat upon a saucer looking bit
By bit intact. Few lines were visible
Except through close inspection. Still, no tea
Was poured into this prized receptacle.
Who knew if it would hold sufficiently?
The precious gift remained unused. Around
It other fragile vessels daily served
All their intended purposes, proved sound
Or were discarded, owner not unnerved.
Just once before had form meant far too much;
She knew that little ever came from such.

Faute de Mieux

Perfection is impossible to find:
We think, "Oh, yes!" then "No!" then "Never mind."

Sometimes we settle for the good enough:
To live with disappointment can be tough.

At other times we go with the less bad:
We later learn, again, we have been had.

Weavings

regarding the series of tapestries at the Musée National du Moyen Âge

The lovely lady looks forlorn
Despite her posture and attire,
Her maid and lion and unicorn.

Her hand lets loose her favorite's horn
To hold a bird she might admire
Were she a little less forlorn.

A monkey may be oh-so-torn:
Tidbit or flower? Why inquire
Of maid or lion or unicorn?

Some organ music has been sworn
To make a day seem more entire,
A lovely lady less forlorn.

If hours come to be timeworn,
A mirror shows what can transpire
With maiden, lion, and unicorn.

No necklace ever could adorn
The body to the soul's desire.
What lady longs to stay forlorn,
Dismayed with lion and unicorn?

Knowledge

You peer into the glass at last
    And find a mere reflection
Of what you slowly recognize
    As definite rejection.

The image horribly confirms
    A dimly-lit suspicion
That you may surely doubt your sight
    But not your intuition.

Rembrandt

Why did a man, unhandsome, often turn
to painting from a mirror? Was he vain,
or not, to focus on someone so plain?
What made an eager spender choose to spurn
a model's fee? Did earnest students learn
more easily to copy the mundane?
Were good commissions hard enough to gain
that money was a matter of concern?

Could he have known that these original
self-portraits would be counted treasures all
in due time? What a record of resilience—
such talent, soon of age, then elderly—
each face illuminated with a brilliance
against the shadows of obscurity.

Chanel

No one but Coco would have thought
Of such designs so often sought.

Hat, handbag, sweater, suit, or dress,
Most every style had great success.

Her clientele could not consume
Enough of No. 5 perfume.

Each item in her chic boutique
Made all who wore it feel unique.

However priced, her haute couture
Possessed a powerful allure.

Though she has passed, her name today
Lives on—but carries less cachet.

Woman of Uncertain Age

It is so hard to tell
if time just treats her well
or if some work was done
since she admits to none.

Her figure is quite fit,
though bosom sags a bit;
her posture is upright,
yet face looks slightly tight.

Her nails are long and sleek,
her clothing is très chic,
but it has been a while
since that hair was in style.

I can but speculate
about her true birthdate;
if I should ask her past,
that line would be my last.

And efforts less direct
yield much the same effect,
for what she offers then
shaves off a year or ten.

From the Palace

by George Alexander Louis

Oh, boy—a girl! A little sister. Swell.
For me, this happening does not bode well.

I am the prince, first-born, the apple of
My parents' eyes, the first fruit of their love.

But now? Am I supposed to learn to say,
"Well, darling Charlotte, would you like to play?"

She eats, she sleeps, she cries. (Her other names
I cannot get.) She is too young for games.

Need I remind the world I am the heir?
Charlotte et cetera is just a spare.

Britannia

As times turned hard and harder yet,
    The Queen grew apprehensive—
Relentless tides of change had made
    One luxury expensive.

Reluctantly, she let her yacht
    Retire to Edinburgh—
It was refitted for a tour
    Both riveting and thorough.

The spaces where the crew once stayed
    Provide much satisfaction—
The ones reserved for royalty
    Surpass them in attraction.

All those who want to get on board
    Are charged the going rate—
Pounds sterling must be spent to see
    How Windsors lived in state.

Railings

Approaching fifty, I indulged the notion
to buy a nifty condo near the ocean.

The third-floor unit, which I dearly love,
has others on both sides, beneath, above.

No person on a balcony is seen
since walls discreetly block each view between.

Aroma, though, from neighboring cigar
drifts dreadfully, however close or far.

Plus, private conversations can be heard
by any resident or guest or bird.

Communal living might be over-rated—
yes, even when the property is gated.

Out of the Bag

Too often I make purchases
    Without a second thought,
Until I get the items home
    And look at what I bought.

If then I find that anything
    Has lost its prior appeal,
The blame goes to the clearance tag
    Which sold me such a deal.

Ipso Facto

The papers came at last: the deal was done,
tried, juried, judged, recorded, stamped in red—
the dissolution of ourselves as one;
that marriage never happened, so they said.

All went into a drawer. Life resumed,
unshared, a continent apart. No traces
of any former union ever loomed
except in each of our four children's faces.

Now grown, those offspring still negotiate
our separate worlds while trying to arrange
their own. They know a lot and speculate
about the rest; thus, credits, debits change.

Some memories remain: the past can seem
too present in an unexpected dream.

Strategy

Encountering an ex again,
Avoid all talk of there and then.

Speak only of the here and now;
If ex should balk, show him/her how.

Be sure to shun the question "why?"
(Its answer often is a lie.)

Maintain some semblance of composure;
Abandon any hope of closure.

Hiatus

My only Muse, I let you take a break,
Not that you asked, but still you were supposed
To come back soon. I cannot take the ache
Of longer absence. Have you played or dozed,
Perhaps found someone else and proved untrue?
Since my ideas are unremarkable
And my next book has gaps, I do need you
To offer thoughts more inspirational.
Do you not miss me? Maybe just a bit?
We had our moments, right? In fact, much fun
For many years! Why would you ever quit
What worked? Is our collaboration done?
To stay away would be a big mistake;
Return to me at once, for goodness' sake.

Detritus

post-consult

There is so little left
of what had been
long-crafted.

The many words lined out
make that work look
just-drafted.

Papier-Mâché

You take offense that I have deigned to throw
Away what you constructed in sixth grade?
Or was it eighth? Does either of us know?
It was indeed a dragon, nicely made,
With layer upon layer well-applied,
Dried, then shellacked, soft tissue-paper flame
Erupting from its mouth. At least I tried
To keep such closeted for years. My aim?
Kind co-existence, not a melding of
Our hands or hearts or minds or else. I raised
You, day by day, only to learn that love
Enacted faithfully may go unpraised
And unreturned. A truly artful life
Transcends the empty selfishness of strife.

Jive Dive

This place gets busy in July.
We stand inside, three of us, queued,
Waiting and watching passersby.

Once seated, oh-so-hungry, dry,
We long to order drinks and food.
This place gets busy in July.

With menu too-well-viewed, we try
To flag down any dame or dude
But watch as waiters pass us by.

With order placed at last, we vie
To see who has the least bad mood.
This place gets busy in July.

When served ('bout time!), we satisfy
Ourselves till all is sipped or chewed,
Then wait and watch those passing by.

To get the bill run, paid, we sigh
And signal, nothing rude or crude.
This place gets busy in July.
Wait! Watch us pass on a goodbye.

The Brouhaha Re: Panama

The media are cutting capers
About a certain cache of papers.

Day after day some wealthy codger
Is shown to be a cagey dodger.

With each embarrassing disclosure
Another pooh-bah fears exposure.

In these lean times all tax evaders
Appear to be no more than traitors.

Dear George,

If only you were living at this hour,
Day, week, month, year. These times are newly strange—
Hilarious, but not. You had prime power
To forge a nation, though within the range
Of law. Good whisky and false teeth might help
Us muddle through an age without decorum,
As candidates bite both their thumbs or yelp
Outrageous claims. With each and every forum
Intemperate behavior seems to spur
Support! Since no one sounds a louder note
Than some audacious trumpeter, which sir
Or madam, native born, deserves my vote?
Tell me, is my best recourse to complain
Or to abstain? Your second cousin, Jane

Mama Drama

A son of mine did what I feared—
He left my house and grew a beard.

He learned to handle life alone—
Then found a girl to call his own.

Soon independence fell to whim—
He let her give his beard a trim.

He never did the same again—
I do consider that a win.

Hegemony

There looms an even larger crisis
Than Panama or Trump or ISIS:
Crustaceans from America
Have caused this latest brouhaha.

Each male is said to have a pincher
So big that it becomes the clincher
In rituals with European
She-lobsters during mating season.

The offspring, though, researchers tell,
May suffer from a thinner shell
Than is ideal to thrive beyond
The western regions of the pond.

So what to do? Why, pass some laws
Against *Homari* with such claws!

André Bénard

(1922–2016)

For eight years he co-led the effort to
construct the Eurotunnel. Problems grew—
political agenda, technical
delays, financial strains, irascible
investors. Decades spent employed at Shell
enabled him to work with others well,
yet his best efforts in diplomacy
could not stop charges of duplicity,
a French investigation, then a trial
with an acquittal. Was all worth his while?
From start to finish, he had doubts but got
"the damn thing" done, a feat which meant a lot
to England. Honored with a knighthood, he
retired to olive trees and poetry.

All We Like Sheep

A statue of the risen Lord,
    No more than four feet tall,
Composed of resin painted gold,
    Hung on the church's wall.

Arms raised, it welcomed everyone
    Approaching from the east:
Saints, sinners, strangers, members, guests,
    The greatest to the least.

One night the statue disappeared
    From its appointed spot;
Months later what was lost was found
    Abandoned in a lot.

It had been tortured by the thieves
    Deprived of some quick sale;
Come final judgment Christ Himself
    Will get to hear their tale.

Until then, He may sigh and say,
    "They know not what they do."
For all, including you and me,
    That is too often true.

Natural Disaster

Cameroon, 1986

The lake was calm above the cloud
that grew unseen, unheard. A loud
mid-summer storm brought lots of rain
as well as rocks, breaking the plane
of Nyos. Gas became a shroud
for thousands, livestock mostly cowed
by boredom, farmers duly proud
of crops, since long in this domain
the lake was calm.
A plethora of experts ploughed
up theories why and how the crowd
had suffered sudden death. Arcane
such seemed to those who could regain
their fields. These came back home, avowed
the lake was calm.

Pathos

Too many media these days
    Call situations "tragic"
So that the word itself can work
    With undetected magic

On those who may or may not know
    Its ancient definition
But undergo catharsis at
    Each current repetition.

Old New World

That warm Atlantic waters rise
Would likely have been no surprise
To those who lived where Jamestown lies.

The settlers there had lots to fear
From more than weather year by year:
Some threat was always much too near.

Starvation, warfare, or disease
Kept these Virginians ill at ease
And often dropped them to their knees.

Today what good is mere remorse
That any oceanic force
Completes its ruin in due course?

Historicism

When what is new becomes the rage
And what is old has lost its charm,
Then renovators set the stage
For changes causing much alarm

To preservationists who think
Such business should be left alone,
Unless their help is hired (*wink, wink*)
On matters really not their own.

Belatedly, a Sonnet

Today I took the time to write about
what happened long ago—our brief romance,
its ending too abrupt perhaps, no doubt
the consequence of choice and circumstance.

We run into each other on occasion;
alone or not, we stop to speak and smile,
then soon depart with obvious evasion
of explanations that would take a while.

Mine could be short: I came to realize,
for both our sakes, that we were not a match
in much of anything, that compromise,
or worse, made neither one of us a catch.

If you should ask: Why now? Why write at all?
I guess not doing so, at last, felt small.

Just Saying

The pundits pause
at this impasse:
The voters may
stay home en masse.

Faith

The first warm day in quite a spell the old
cat wandered off. She had been ailing for
weeks, eating little, less, and then no more.
She somehow knew the end was near—and told
us that—but still we trusted her to leave
and to return as usual. When she
did not, the yard was searched extensively—
morn, noon, and night. We could not start to grieve
as long as we believed she would be found.
The third day there she was—back home for good—
curled up, eyes wide. We did all that we should—
a simple burial in sandy ground
not far from where we come and go a lot.
A mottled fieldstone marks the very spot.

Manifesto

Fifty and a hundred years
should have dried all Southern tears.
Raze the plaques and monuments
honoring long-gone events.
Tip the statues of the men
uniformed in gray back then.
Put away the battle flag;
let it neither fly nor swag.
Desecrate the graves of those
whose beliefs most now oppose.
Never read or sing a verse
that could cause a scene or worse.
Rid from any memory
relics of Confederacy.

Storage

What good is any heirloom locked
    inside a special closet?

How valuable is something stashed
    away in safe-deposit?

Why own a treasure only to
    be scared that you will lose it?

Is anything worth keeping if
    you never dare to use it?

Abode

Awkward is how I feel when entering
a house no longer mine. Too much has changed—
paint, paper, carpet with the opening
of once-closed rooms, their confines re-arranged
and filled with furniture I neither chose
nor bought. A mounted television, on
low volume during my brief visit, shows
high-definition sports. Nothing bon-ton
demands attention, just the normal stuff
of daily life—books, cushions, lamps, knick-knacks,
clocks, candles, potted plants, more than enough
in place or out to make most guests relax.
But strangely I do not become less tense
until I leave—again—this residence.

RIP, Antonin Scalia

Reportedly, his heart gave out,
But rumor starts, then gets about.

The Justice was found dead in bed,
A pillow somewhere near his head.

Was such "above" or "on" his face?
So much depends upon the place.

At least his host has shown contrition
For wrongful use of preposition.

Quid Pro Quo

It is so hard to write and then arrange
a partial or a full collection, not
to mention two or three, but fair exchange
with people in the biz can help a lot.
Advice on verse, entrée to publications,
reviews, awards, gigs, grants—when mutual—
have benefits, establish reputations,
and make more of the same more possible.
Reclusive types must push themselves to learn
the art of trading opportunity
with others if they ever are to earn
a modest profit from their poetry.
This common strategy should work just fine:
"Look here, I'll scratch your back if you'll scratch mine."

Ordeal

When my back went from bad to worse
    And I could hardly walk,
It seemed that everyone I knew
    Felt some strange urge to talk.

I listened very patiently
    To non-expert advice;
Some folks insisted heat would work,
    Yet others spoke of ice.

One doctor ordered medicine
    Despite the common risk;
Another swore no pill would fix
    A herniated disc.

A third complained my painful case
    Was lasting far too long;
His words did little more than prove
    My treatment had gone wrong.

Awaiting micro-surgery,
    I tried to pose as bold;
My long-grown daughter made the point,
    "You're too young to be old."

The day before the hospital,
    My spirits got quite low;
My husband then encouraged me,
    "You don't have long to go."

I did survive and soon went home
    To rest in my own bed;
My goal was to recover from
    What had been done and said.

Post-Op

So slow is my recovery
That it is hard to feel like me.

If only back (and mind) could bend,
I would be quicker on the mend.

Rate

Listen! Do you hear it? Count the
chirps it makes in fourteen seconds,
then add forty—there you have the
temperature in Fahrenheit.

Evidently such a method
works precisely with the crickets
known as snowy, partial to trees.

But results may vary with the
species fond of fields, where factors
such as age and mating matter.

Maybe Dolbear's law applies to
poets—most of us who filter
life for inspiration do chirp
faster as the air gets hotter.

dos-à-dos

"Oh, no, it can't be him again," I think
while following the hostess to a booth.
Of course, he spots me, grins, and gives a wink
as if such manners made him less uncouth.
I fake a smile, then tell two lies: "So good
to see you! Hope you're doing well!" I've got
to sit behind him. Friend ("How could she?") would
have placed herself already. "It's too hot
in here," she comments, with a smirk. "Indeed,"
I say ("You witch!"), then order, "Unsweet tea
with lemon, trio salad, no chickweed."
Her? "Steak, rare, wedge with ranch, not fat-free,
and water." Leaning forward I can munch,
sip, talk, try not to listen. There goes lunch.

Accommodation

Of any beauty I once had
There is too little left;
Despite this unattractive fact,
I do not feel bereft.

My doting spouse seems not to mind
I have grown plainly old;
His eyes have gotten weaker since
He first did me behold.

Nest

My foot sank deep into the ground, and out
swarmed yellow jackets. I was stung by two
before I could start running. By the time
I reached the house, a third had hit me hard;
more followed me inside. Off came my shirt
to whack at those that buzzed around the door,
slammed shut, till bodies fell and lay there. Safe,
I stuck an arm into a sleeve and found
one devil hiding yet. I killed it, too.

Through summer into autumn others left
the nest, returned at will. I stayed away,
reluctant to get close enough to douse
the hole with any poison. Wasp by wasp
went after roses, then sasanquas just
outside the kitchen window, where I watched
them hover, have whatever blossoms that
they wanted. Colder weather would take care
of all except the queen: she would be mine.

Cotillion

So here we are again
at yet another *fête,*
just sitting by ourselves
and talking *tête-à-tête.*

Though most will take a turn
to spin in this *milieu,*
let's wait till we get home
to dance a *pas de deux.*

Rhyme after Rime

The Wedding-Guest awoke to find
Himself in his own bed;
He wasn't sure which ached him more—
His stomach or his head.

He told the Bridesmaid by his side,
"Get up and fetch an egg."
When she rolled over, he complained,
"I shouldn't have to beg."

She rose, put on her dress, then left
To see what she could do;
Returning soon, she offered him,
"No egg, but this in lieu."

His fav'rite hen! Its neck just wrung!
He was too shocked to curse:
"Thank God I never pledged my troth
For better or for worse."

Admonition

Should lover look or act contrary
To usual and customary
Much longer than a shift in humor,
The reason seldom is a tumor.

More likely he or she has taken
Another lover, you forsaken,
So pay attention to such changes
And be the first who rearranges.

By and By

"In the resurrection . . . whose wife will the woman be?"
—Luke 20:33a

Should I be worthy of a second birth
I shall remain a virgin. Husbands may
Sometimes prove helpful in this stint on earth
But never later. When the blessèd day
Arrives that Christ, the Lord, returns at last,
I need not fall in love or out. No man
Will lift me up to lay me down, soon cast
Me off to satisfy himself. I can
Be whole again, stay newly made, and lack
For nothing—ever. Meanwhile, I pray, wait,
Repeat the selfsame dream of looking back
And forth to find who is my current mate.
Beyond the here and now is death that leads
To life illimited by human needs.

At Church on Christmas Day

A solitary goldfish lay
    Beneath the common pew;
It was the sort of cracker which
    A child would want to chew.

The fact that no foot crushed it in
    The crowd the night before
Seemed yet another miracle,
    As if we needed more.

In Toto

*regarding the cookies sold
by Girl Scouts in the USA
each winter to raise funds*

The problem with Thin Mints, you see,
Is that they cause obesity.

I buy a box, draw out a sleeve,
Consume a few, then fail to leave

The rest for yet another time
Since all should go while in their prime.

Why let a single one get stale?
Thus ends this cautionary tale.

Or not. Sleeve two is opened soon.
So, Thin Mint versus Lorna Doone?

I read fine print for calories.
The latter has far fewer? Please!

What does that really matter now?
Those Scouts have snookered me somehow.

Willy-Nilly

Inserting some fresh dollar bill,
You punch the proper button for
A candy bar, which moves until
It stops, hung up, and moves no more.

You wait for what may happen yet,
Just as you have with parenthood:
You paid for what you may not get,
For reasons never understood.

At the Cincinnati Zoo

[28 May 2016]

[Mother]

Oh me oh my
I daily try

To do my best
To pass each test

However odd
A child or God

[Onlooker]

Some creatures are
Too wild by far

[Son]

I want to go
But Mom says no

So I will sneak
To take a peek

Since it is fun
To make her run

[Employee]

I could aim at
The ape or brat

[Harambe]

When that boy fell
Into my well

I came about
And checked him out

Until a shot
Cost me a lot

Drill

The quick brown fox jumps over the lazy dog.
 —common pangram

What if the lazy dog jumped up and chased
the quick brown fox out of the yard? Type that
for extra credit if you dare! Hands placed
and fingers poised? Go! . . . Hmm, not quite down pat.
Good effort, but you might do better if
you practiced more. I know, I know, today
thumbs are the means to text a verbal riff;
voice recognition software is the way
to turn ideas into documents.
The keyboard, though, is not yet obsolete;
technology, like teaching, re-invents
itself, and your coursework is incomplete.
Regardless of what happens out of class,
you must type well enough in here to pass.

Otology

The drive is easy early in the day—
ten minutes tops—ten more to park. I walk
into the building, find the office well
before eight-thirty. The reception room
is far from full. I choose an empty chair,
fill out too many forms, and wait—all set.

A nurse soon guides me back to where I set
aside belongings. Vital signs today
are excellent. Moved to another chair,
I answer questions, see the doctor walk
up/down the hall. He comes into the room,
asks how I am. I simply say, "Unwell."

"And why is that?" he counters, then bids, "Well,
let's take a look." I hesitantly set
myself upon a cushioned slab. The room
becomes a torture chamber. "Oh, Monday,
Monday, so good to me," I mutely walk
through lyrics till I get back to a chair.

Next I am moved to yet another chair
inside a lab designed to test how well
I hear. The nurse and the computer walk
me through procedure. Earplugs in, headset
and collar on, I click a pen all day
or so it seems—tone/pulse—in that strange room.

At last the nurse comes back into the room,
adjusts something. I must stay in the chair,
touch squares within a grid to show "birthday"
is not "rainbow," "football" is not "inkwell,"
"toothbrush" is not "mousetrap." The sound is set
too low: "padlock"? "horseshoe"? maybe "sidewalk"?

The test advances. Rhymes are a cakewalk
compared to spondees. Yes, I own the room
throughout this section. Volume has been set
so I can choose one out of four. The chair
feels almost comfortable as I do well.
Perhaps I might survive this endless day.

Back in the other room, I take a chair,
hear wins have offset losses, say farewell,
rise and walk out into the still-young day.

Another Spring

"Pyros, the alpha bear of the Pyrenees, is on the move again."
—The Wall Street Journal

Both French and Spanish specialists are vexed
Because a certain bear is oversexed.

Brought from Slovenia in '87,
He made this mountain range his randy heaven.

Pyros became extremely lecherous;
Ursine relations turned incestuous.

Officials now concerned about genetics
Bemoan their own Lothario's athletics.

Admirers, though, consider it unfair
To criticize a legendary bear.

No lover lasts forever; time will tell
When Pyros stops performing quite so well.

Annulment

You offered to become my beau forever—
I trusted you to love me so forever.

A ceremony happened in a church—
We promised unity, weal/woe, forever.

The honeymoon was oddly interrupted—
I thought the marriage still would go forever.

We had five pregnancies in thirteen years—
Too bad I could not keep the glow forever.

A major difference always was apparent—
You fancied fast, I favored slow, forever.

I tired of talk and longed to settle down—
You did not want that status quo forever.

You left for other women, other places—
Who cared if you turned fiend and foe forever?

The monthly checks for children finally stopped—
You never can pay what you owe forever.

Post-reckoning all recollection ends—
It is not you whom Jane will know forever.

Artificial Intelligence

For months I manage to defer updating my
computer to relentless Windows 10, but then
one random morning nothing I can think to try
will interrupt an automated process. When
percentages show Microsoft's all done, I'm left
to reconfigure browsers just to access sites
long designated favorites. Totally bereft
of choice throughout the whole ordeal, I feel my rights
have been abridged, if violated is too strong
a term. How much control must I surrender to
such forces just to get online? Is it so wrong
of me to be reluctant to accept what's new?
With most change, doesn't timing matter? Rote words sting
as up pops, "I'm Cortana. Ask me anything."

A Question of Critique

When one has tried—and done—a lot,
Who wants to hear, "You missed a spot"?

Meeting at the Sewanee Inn

"The six-daies world transposing in an houre . . ."
—George Herbert in "Prayer (1)"

It lasted only thirty minutes and
took place on Sunday, but the metaphor
works well enough. My presence was unplanned.
I simply wanted breakfast—eggs, ham or
bacon, grits, tea. A door was open down
the hall—housekeepers sat around a table—
a voice intoned a lesson—not a frown
appeared on any face. Struck, I was able
to pause just past the threshold. Hunger made
me leave too quickly—plus, the awkwardness
of listening uninvited. If I had stayed,
would I be more articulate? God bless
us all: the ones who write or sing a hymn;
those who make beds or have to lie in them.

Ossuary

Each time I toss or turn I seem
To have the same unpleasant dream.

I walk through—not a fine museum—
But some macabre mausoleum.

The rooms I pass are full of bones—
None coming from long-gone unknowns.

These ossified remains belong
To those who chose to do me wrong.

Only if such has been confessed
Can bones transform from cursed to blessed.

May flesh and blood bring me release
From all that is averse to peace.

Voice Mail

You have called the very phone
That I choose to keep my own
With a number undisclosed.

Leave a message if you will
Should you want to reach me still
When I am less indisposed.

Contra Naturam

The same old fights resume each day
As mockingbirds scare crows away.

Wings flap so fast that feathers blur
When breakfast brings a predator.

Each species tries to save its nest
From raiders at their hungry best.

Thus, even sparrows make a fuss
When mealtime turns to them or us.

This primal urge to save one's own
Does not exist in birds alone.

Most parents have an inner drive
To help offspring survive and thrive.

Things seldom do get so messed up
That hatchlings serve as hatchers' sup.

Foregone

My father's time did come. He had to die.
Procedures and precautions—lots—delayed
The date, but even he could neither buy
Nor bully brute mortality. He stayed
Too long at home, designed and built and paid
For brilliantly—or so he bragged. His kin
Would seldom visit. Neighbors were afraid
To do much more than notice if or when
The yard man or the maid appeared. Again
And yet again the mail would be retrieved,
The trash set out. Routine and normal. Then
I heard he was removed—next, I bereaved.
The shock was that I could not shed a tear.
I had already mourned some yesteryear.

Cut

Most people wait their turn in line;
They mutter maybe, even whine,

But one man does not give a hoot
About the ordinary route.

When visiting a funeral home,
He steps inside, lets his eyes roam

Till he finds folks familiar there,
Whom he may join, as on a dare.

Then he walks up and stops to chat,
With hope none cares about all that.

Thus, he can pay his due respect.
What else could anyone expect?

Comparison

There is so little comfort in the fact
That someone else has felt such misery;
The similarity may prove exact,
But I have never loved much company.

Instead I would prefer to be unique
In owning up to agony extreme;
Results of any contest would be bleak
Without the listing of my name supreme.

Those fools who beg to differ can go hang
Themselves on threads of sayings over ages;
May this rebuttal serve as my harangue
Against advice of cockamamie sages.

An aphorism all too often fails:
No easy fix exists to cure what ails.

Forthwith

Wise men, women, children, too,
Follow still the sacred light
First appearing on the night
When a virgin's son came due.

Thus, the prophecy proved true:
Bethlehem would be the site
Where a king or shepherd might
See how hope is born anew.

Now as then, the person who
Seeks relief from any plight
Finds that neither depth nor height
Keeps this star from shining through.

Au Naturel

"Naked I came from my mother's womb, and naked shall I return; the LORD gave, and the LORD has taken away; blessed be the name of the LORD."

—Job 1:21

God gives and takes, and so life goes,
And mine has led me to conclude
There often is no need for clothes.

A person starts, then grows, then slows,
As mind and body get tattooed;
God gives and takes, and so life goes.

Whatever be the plan or pose,
The time or place, the mode or mood,
There often is no need for clothes.

A self-examination shows
I look my best—and worst—when nude;
God gives and takes, and so life goes.

Each age or stage has thrills and throes;
In company or solitude
There often is no need for clothes.

The greatest wisdom comes from those
Who know truth may be misconstrued:
God gives and takes, and so life goes;
There often is no need for clothes.

Testament

Lay me out in lavender—
Place a lily in one hand—
Let a single finger stay
Circled by a wedding band.

Summon some good minister—
Gather a few family—
Pray that God may keep my soul
Safe for all eternity.

Sing a song and raise a glass—
Go for yet another round—
Think of me as she who rests
Happily in hallowed ground.

Living Will

after Shakespeare's Sonnet 71

You better mourn for me when I am dead,
Hope I have gone to Heaven, not to Hell,
Feel oddly small in our large marriage bed,
Miss all the ways I loved and served you well.
In fact, you should remember me a lot
When reading what I crafted years ago
Or much more recently, perhaps a jot
About some such-and-such to so-and-so.
Once I have been transported by a hearse
To rest beneath the sod, await the day
When we again, for better or for worse,
Lie side by side as worms waste us away,
   Let others note that you may moan and groan
   Yet are content to sleep (or not) alone.

Memoir

Remembering isn't necessarily easy.
Exactly what did happen?
With whom?
And when?
Not to mention where?
Since recollection comes in bits and pieces,
A record of a lifetime is a mere collage,
A scrapbook cluttered with cards
And tickets and pictures,
A mosaic of shards and slivers
Distorting the image in the mirror.
How does one arrange the fragments of the past
In order to represent the truth of
What was, what is, and what will be?
Remembering isn't necessarily easy.
But neither is forgetting.

About the Author

A native Virginian, Jane Blanchard lives and writes in Georgia. She has five previous collections—*Never Enough Already* (2021), *In or Out of Season* (2020), *After Before* (2019), *Tides & Currents* (2017), and *Unloosed* (2016)—all with Kelsay Books.